THE CHANGING FACE OF
SOUTH AFRICA

TONY BINNS and ROB BOWDEN

RAINTREE
STECK-VAUGHN
RSVP PUBLISHERS

A Harcourt Company

Austin   New York
www.raintreesteckvaughn.com

Published by Raintree Steck-Vaughn Publishers, an imprint of Steck-Vaughn Company

Library of Congress Cataloging-in-Publication Data is available upon request.

ISBN 0-7398-4968-9

Printed in Italy. Bound in the United States.

1 2 3 4 5 6 7 8 9 0 LB 06 05 04 03 02

Acknowledgments

All photographs are by Tony Binns except: Diamond Promotion Service 12; Hodder Wayland/Gordon Clements 17, 25, 37, 39; Panos 21 (lower); Popperfoto 7 (lower), 29 (top). Statistics panel illustrations are by Nick Hawken. The map (page 8) is by Peter Bull.

Contents

1 "City of Gold"

The city of Johannesburg is a city built on gold. In 1886 gold was discovered on the nearby Witwatersrand, and thousands of people flocked to the area hoping to make their fortunes. Many did become rich—but these were mainly the white mine owners. For the black workers who came to Johannesburg, there was only hard work in the mines and a rough life in the camps, far from their families.

Throughout the 20th century, the lives of black and of white South Africans were very different. In 1948 the white government set up a system called "apartheid," which made the lives of black people even harder. But in 1994, apartheid came to an end. South Africa became known as the "Rainbow Nation," with the rainbow as a symbol and celebration of the variety of people who make up its population.

Johannesburg today is a thriving modern city, the second biggest in South Africa and home to 2.5 million people. However, new supplies of gold are becoming harder and more expensive to find. The price that international traders pay for gold is falling.

▲ *A busy market in a Johannesburg street.*

▶ *Today, these children go to the same school. During the apartheid years, white and Asian children had to attend separate schools.*

Many gold mines have closed and people have lost their jobs. Crime is rising. In Johannesburg, as in the rest of South Africa, the end of apartheid has brought many changes and new challenges.

▲ *Johannesburg is Africa's most important financial center.*

SOUTH AFRICA: KEY FACTS

Area: 470,000 square miles (1,219,090 sq km)

Population: 40.5 million (1996 census); mid-1999 estimate = 43.5 million

Population density: 14 people per square mile (36 people per sq km)

Capitals: Pretoria (administrative, 1.25 million), Bloemfontein (judicial, 0.15 million) and Cape Town (legislative, 2.55 million)

Other main cities: Johannesburg (2.5 million), Durban (2.5 million), Port Elizabeth (0.95 million)

Highest mountain: Thabana Ntlenyana 2 miles or 3,800 yards (3,482 m)

Longest river: Orange 1,292 miles (2,080 km)

Main languages: Afrikaans, English and 9 African languages

Major religions: Christianity (66%), traditional beliefs (30%), Hinduism (1%), Islam (1%), others (2%)

Currency: Rand (100 cents = 1 Rand)

Sources: *Britannica Yearbook 2000; South Africa: Past, Present and Future.*

Past Times

European settlers first arrived in what is now Cape Town in 1652. These early settlers were farmers and a struggle for land soon developed between them and the native black population. In 1871, diamonds were discovered at Kimberley and in 1886, gold deposits were found near Johannesburg. Thousands more Europeans arrived, hoping to make money from the mining industry. South Africa became the richest country in Africa. The white population quickly used its wealth to take control of the land and people.

The Apartheid Era

In 1948 the white South African government introduced a policy called "apartheid." Apartheid means "to keep apart," and the new policy was a deliberate attempt to separate white and black people. Apartheid laws governed almost every aspect of people's lives, from where they could live, to the park benches they could sit on. Black people had to carry a government pass at all times; if they did not, they could be arrested.

Black groups such as the African National Congress (ANC) began campaigns against apartheid. But the government resisted, often with violent results. In one of the worst incidents, 69 protesters were shot dead and another 180 were wounded by police in Sharpeville in March 1960. Many black leaders were imprisoned. One of these leaders, Nelson Mandela, became an international symbol of the struggle of black South Africans to be treated equally.

Continued violence and pressure from countries that refused to trade with South Africa eventually led to Mandela's release in 1990. Apartheid was ended in 1991 and in April 1994, all South Africans were allowed to vote for the first time. Nelson Mandela was elected president.

▲ A statue of a Dutch farmer's wife and her children on the Voortrekker Monument in Pretoria. This monument was set up to commemorate the Battle of Blood River in 1838, when Dutch settlers searching for new lands defeated Zulus.

IN THEIR OWN WORDS

"My name is Elias and I am standing outside Robben Island prison—you can see the bars on the windows behind me. I was imprisoned here during the apartheid years, along with many of my fellow countrymen. One of the most famous prisoners here was Nelson Mandela, who became our president after his release. During our time here we worked in the quarry, breaking stones by hand. It was very hard work and working in the bright sunshine every day damaged our eyes because of the reflection from the rocks. Today the prison is a tourist attraction. I work here as a guide, telling tourists about apartheid and the way we were treated."

▼ Nelson Mandela (center) during the ceremony at which he was sworn in as president of South Africa, in 1994. His successor, Thabo Mbeki, is on the left and Mandela's daughter Zinani is on the right.

3 Landscape and Climate

South Africa is the tenth-largest country in Africa. It takes up the whole of the southern tip of the continent. It is almost twice the size of Texas, and over five times bigger than the United Kingdom. South Africa's landscape and climate are extremely varied, ranging from hot, dry deserts to cool, wet mountains.

The Great Escarpment

Running down nearly the entire country, a line of mountains called the "Great Escarpment" dominates the landscape like a giant backbone. The Drakensberg (Dragon) Mountains on the border between Lesotho (a mountain kingdom entirely surrounded by South Africa) and Kwazulu Natal are the most impressive part of the escarpment.

▼ *This map shows the main features of the South African landscape and the major cities. Places mentioned in this book are also shown.*

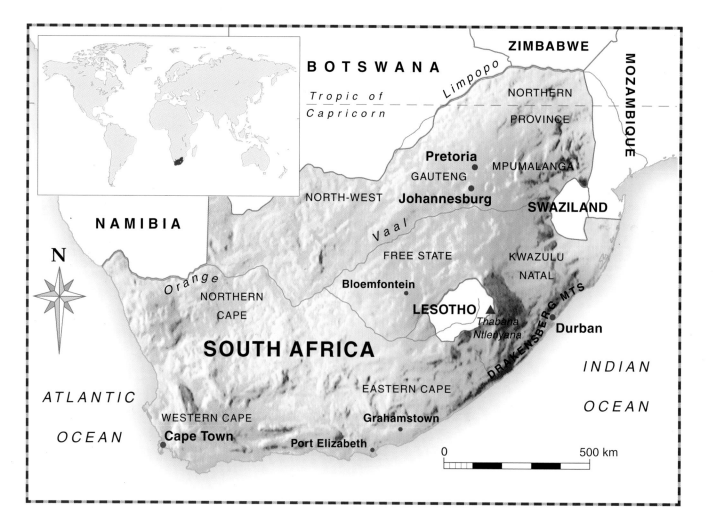

South Africa's best-known mountain is Table Mountain, which overlooks the city of Cape Town. This beautiful flat-topped mountain is a famous landmark and is often covered by a layer of clouds, like a giant tablecloth.

The mountains are, on average, 57°F (12°C) cooler than lower-lying areas, and the Drakensberg region may have 150 frosty days each year. Rainfall is higher in the mountains too, although it only exceeds 31.5 inches (800 mm) per year in the eastern part of the country. People who live in the mountains herd animals such as goats and cattle, and grow crops such as corn on the fertile slopes facing the coast.

▲ *Table Mountain towers over Cape Town. It can be seen by sailors many miles out at sea and marks the dangerous waters around the Cape of Good Hope.*

IN THEIR OWN WORDS

"My name is Alice and this is my daughter, Thandi (*right*). We live here in Mpofu district, Eastern Cape. This year our corn is growing well because the rains were good, but we are not always so fortunate. The land is dry—ideal for plants like the cacti and sisal you can see behind me, but not very good for crops! In years when there is not much rain, we sometimes struggle to grow enough crops to feed ourselves. We have some goats and chickens and we can sell these to buy food, or we eat them ourselves. If we have droughts as bad as the one in 1998, we sometimes have to reduce the amount we eat each day."

The Highlands

Two-thirds of South Africa is made up of an area of high land that is often called the "highveld." The Orange River runs through the highlands from the mountains to the Atlantic Ocean. It forms the border with Namibia on the last part of its journey. The Great Escarpment prevents moist air from the oceans reaching the highlands, so there is less than 23.6 inches (600 mm) of rainfall per year in this region. People living here face the threat of drought, although too much water can also be a problem in some years. Northern Cape is the driest province—less than 7.9 inches (200 mm) of rain per year and summer temperatures of well over 86 °F (30 °C) are normal. Few people can survive in such hot and dry conditions, and only 2 percent of South Africa's population lives here.

▲ *These granite rock formations are in the Swartberg Mountains in Western Cape province. They are known as* koppies.

IN THEIR OWN WORDS

"I'm Karel and I run a small vineyard near Montagu in Western Cape. The soil and climate are good for producing wine in this region. The biggest vineyards are around Stellenbosch, further west, but here I produce specialty sweet white wines. Since the end of apartheid, we have been able to sell our wine all over the world and we have expanded to meet the demand. Here I am checking that the vines have been tied properly. If they are not tied, the weight of the grapes can break the vines and ruin the crop. There's a bigger risk of this happening if we get heavy rain storms as the grapes are maturing—so I'm not taking any chances!"

The Lowlands and Coastal Plain

The low-lying land at the edges of the highland is known as the "lowveld." There is also a narrow strip of lowland around the coast. In the west the lowlands are desert-like. To the east of Cape Town, there is rich soil. The weather here is warm and there are good amounts of rainfall. This area is ideal for growing crops; many of South Africa's vineyards and fruit farms are here.

In the extreme east around Durban, the climate is more tropical. This area is very popular with tourists, but most people earn their living from agriculture rather than tourism. Several rivers including the Fish, Great Kei, and Tugela flow through this coastal strip to the Indian Ocean. Wetlands just south of Swaziland provide an important habitat for wildlife.

▼ *Vegetables and citrus trees are grown here on the fertile plains near Port Elizabeth in the Eastern Cape.*

4 Natural Resources

Minerals Galore

South Africa has some of the largest and most important mineral reserves in the world. It is the biggest gold producer, supplying almost a quarter of the world total. It has the world's largest reserves of the metals chromium, platinum,

▼ *Workers sorting and grading diamonds.*

manganese, and vanadium. These are used in industry. It is also a major producer of diamonds, coal, and iron ore. Almost half the income South Africa earns from selling goods abroad comes from mining. The mining industry employs almost half a million people.

Deposits of gold are becoming harder to reach, so mining companies are having to rely more on machines to do the work. Tunneling machines can reach a depth of 1.864 miles (3 km) below the surface. Another problem facing the gold-mining industry is that the price international traders pay for gold has been falling. In 1980 an ounce (28g) of gold would sell for $850, but by 1999 an ounce was worth just $250. Gold mining has become less profitable and, as a result, in 1998 gold production in South Africa fell to its lowest level in 42 years. Sixty-four thousand miners lost their jobs.

Although gold production has been falling, the mining of coal and chromium increased during the 1990s. Platinum mining is also expected to increase, following the opening of the new Froondal platinum mine in 1999.

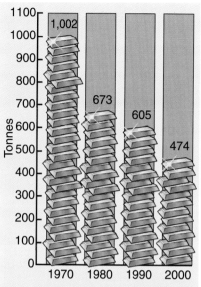

Source: Geographical Digest and Lester, Nel and Binns

▲ *Falling gold production has led to mine closures and job losses for miners.*

IN THEIR OWN WORDS

"My name is Thabo (I'm the one in the yellow hat) and I work in a gold mine near Welkom in Free State. I am originally from Umtata in the former Transkei homeland, but like many of my fellow miners I live away from home for long periods. Some miners come from as far away as Mozambique, Zimbabwe, and even Kenya. I used to work underground, but this was hard and dangerous and we were often injured. I now work on the surface, making sure the machinery that takes miners down to the goldface is running properly. (You can see the machinery behind the trees in this picture.) Many of my friends have lost their jobs as mines have closed. I hope that I will keep my job—I enjoy it and it pays well, though I do miss my family."

Energy

More than 95 percent of South Africa's electricity is supplied by burning fossil fuels. Coal is the most important fuel, as South Africa has reserves that will last for at least 350 years. Nuclear power is used to generate almost all the rest of the country's electricity. Tiny amounts come from hydroelectric power plants and renewable sources such as solar power.

The demand for electricity increased by about 30 percent between 1980 and 1996 and continues to grow rapidly. Government plans are helping more people to have power in their homes—between 1994 and 2000, two million homes were connected to electricity supplies. Unfortunately, many of these homes have since been cut off because the owners cannot afford to pay the bills.

▲ *In rural communities there is very little street lighting. At Hankey in Eastern Cape, solar power is used to light up these mailboxes at night, so that people can see where to get their mail.*

▼ *Here, logs are being piled into a burner, where they will be turned into charcoal. Charcoal is an important fuel for many people.*

Almost 40 percent of homes still have no electricity. Most of these are in the townships, in shanty towns, or in rural areas. People living here use paraffin, charcoal, or wood collected from the local area to provide energy for cooking, heating, and light.

South Africa has some natural gas and in February 1997 it also began oil production at a small oilfield 87 miles (140 km) offshore from Mossel Bay. During the apartheid years, foreign governments refused to sell oil to South Africa, so scientists developed methods of making oil from coal, and petroleum from natural gas.

IN THEIR OWN WORDS

"My name is Simeon (I'm the one in the blue vest) and I am 11 years old. Here I am recycling paper with my classmates, Peter and Ondela. Each classroom has a cardboard bin for us to put our used paper in and at the end of each day a few of us volunteer to empty it into the dumpster. A company called Sappi collects the dumpster about every two weeks. I think it is very important to save resources in this way because it saves energy and helps to protect the environment. I'd like to recycle at home too, but there is nowhere to take the paper. I think we should have dumpsters, like the one at school, so that everyone can help protect our environment."

Wildlife

The value of wildlife and landscapes is often forgotten, but these natural resources help South Africa earn money. Since the end of apartheid, South Africa has become a popular vacation destination. The number of European and American visitors more than doubled between 1994 and 1998 to over 1.2 million a year. Most tourists spend at least a day in a national park and South Africa's national parks are some of the best in Africa.

◀ *An elephant in Addo Elephant Park, Eastern Cape province. Since the end of apartheid, South Africa has been able to profit from its fascinating wildlife.*

IN THEIR OWN WORDS

"I'm Reghard and I'm a game warden in a small private game park. I take groups of visitors on tours of the park, where they can see animals such as giraffes, zebras, and wildebeests (gnus). Most of our visitors are tourists from Europe and America and a lot more of them have been coming in recent years. The government runs the largest national parks, such as Kruger and Addo Elephant Reserve, but smaller privately-owned parks like this one are opening throughout South Africa. Many white farmers are creating parks where people pay up to $80 per day to visit."

The most famous of South Africa's national parks is Kruger National Park on the northeast border with Mozambique and Zimbabwe. This park is as big as Israel and has a variety of environments, each attracting different species. In total there are some 500 bird species, 114 species of reptile, 23,000 species of plants, and 146 species of mammals, including the "big five" (lion, elephant, buffalo, black rhino, and leopard) that most tourists come to see. Around 700,000 people visit Kruger each year.

South Africans have worked hard to promote their country's natural beauty in recent years. Visitors can enjoy whale-watching and seal-watching trips, shark diving, tours to study flowers and plants, and adventure sports such as whitewater rafting. The bravest can try the highest bungee jump in the world—a terrifying 708-foot (216-m) plunge from the Bloukrans River Bridge. These attractions are big moneymakers. Tourists pay to visit or take part in them, and also spend money on food, transportation, accommodations, and souvenirs during their stay.

▼ *A farmer working on her vegetable crop in Gauteng province.*

Land and Water

Much of South Africa is too dry for farming, but it does have some very fertile farmland on the slopes of the Great Escarpment, and large areas of flatter farmland in Free State province. In the Western Cape province in particular there are large orchards of peach and apple trees, and vineyards where grapes are grown. Most of the country is only suitable for raising livestock such as cattle and sheep. South Africa has no major lakes and limited supplies of fresh water. Reservoirs are used to store and supply water for towns and large farms.

5 The Changing Environment

Water Scarcity

The scarcity of water is the main environmental issue in South Africa. Rainfall is low across most of the country, and is also extremely unpredictable. As a result, water shortages and droughts frequently affect the lives of millions of people.

In recent years rainfall has become even more unpredictable. This may be due to the climate change that many scientists believe is taking place across the globe. The burning of fossil fuels releases carbon dioxide into the atmosphere. Vegetation is removed to clear land for building and agriculture so that there are fewer plants to absorb the carbon dioxide. Scientists believe that as carbon dioxide builds up, it traps heat from the earth, causing global warming and changing weather patterns. In South Africa there were long dry periods in the 1990s. A cyclone caused widespread flooding and damage in 2000. Extreme weather like this may be a result of global warming and may become more common in the future.

▼ *This is a camp for refugees from Mozambique. Like many South Africans, these women have to collect water from a well and use as little as possible.*

Creating More Water

In 1995 scientists noticed that it often rained near a paper mill in Mpumalanga province. They discovered that emissions from the mill attracted water in the clouds and encouraged rainfall. In the future it may be possible to "milk the clouds" in other parts of South Africa. This could be done by firing special flares into the clouds, releasing emissions similar to those from the paper mill.

One plan that is already being used to increase water supplies is the "Working for Water" project. The plan removes unwanted trees and other plants that are growing near rivers and streams. This allows more of the water to flow downstream for people to use, rather than being absorbed by the plants.

Plans like these can help a little but are unlikely to solve the problem of water scarcity in the long run, especially as living standards improve and people begin to use more water in their daily lives.

▲ *This man is clearing vegetation as part of the "Working for Water" project in the Eastern Cape.*

IN THEIR OWN WORDS

"My name is Mandilakhe and I'm 12. I look after my family's donkeys—this is one of them. We use the donkeys to collect water from the well. It's hard work and the well is too far away for us to carry the water by hand. My father grows cabbages to sell, and we also use the donkeys to carry the cabbages to the market. Our fields are irrigated—without the irrigation it would be very difficult to grow crops here. I hope that one day we will have piped water like they do in the towns, but I am not sure if this will happen."

Delicate Soil

In many areas of South Africa the soil is not very fertile. White farmers who run commercial farms own the best land. They produce wine, fruit, or other cash crops for export. In contrast most black farmers are crowded into former homelands where the soil is poor. With so many people trying to farm this land and find grazing for their animals, the soil has become eroded. Now fewer and fewer crops can be grown, and the unpredictable climate makes the situation worse. Gullying is a growing problem because there is less vegetation to hold the soil together. In heavy rains the soil is just washed away.

The government is trying to help by giving people land to farm in less crowded areas, but so far few families have been moved. Many farmers already have their own methods of protecting and improving soil. In parts of Northern province, for example, they plant trees to hold the soil together, and many farmers plow their land across slopes (plowing up and down slopes makes it easier for soil to wash away in the rain).

However, as the population continues to grow, and more food is needed, the soil is likely to become more damaged.

▲ *This farm is using irrigation sprinklers to make up for the lack of rainfall, but poor quality soil in much of South Africa still makes it difficult to grow crops.*

IN THEIR OWN WORDS

"My name is Joseph and I live in Messina in Northern province, near the border of Zimbabwe. I am nearly 64 and in my lifetime I have seen many of the trees cleared for land or to provide fuel. Without trees to hold the soil together, it can be washed away in heavy storms or blown away by the wind. Now I am working with the local community to encourage people to plant trees on their land. We have a small nursery that provides seedlings and I visit farmers to explain the benefits of planting trees and how to care for them. The project is still new, but we hope it will improve our farmland in the future and prevent further erosion."

Some experts believe that South Africa is at risk of serious desertification. This is when the soil becomes too poor to grow anything—like deserts. Once an area becomes desertified, it can be very difficult for people to earn a living and they may be forced to move to a different area.

▼ *Deep gullies have formed here in the former homeland of Transkei. This makes it difficult for farmers to work the land.*

Urban Environments

During the apartheid years, housing policies were designed to keep the majority of black people out of towns and cities. As a result, South Africa's urban areas have not grown as quickly as most African cities. However, in 2000 over half of South Africa's population lived in urban areas, and these areas are now growing rapidly. Environmental problems are becoming increasingly critical.

Pollution from vehicles and industry already causes problems such as acid rain, which damages plants and buildings. Streams and rivers suffer from pollution when household and industrial waste is dumped into them. This is a particular problem in shanty towns, where there is often no proper wastewater system. Government and private housing plans have been set up to tackle this problem, and people are working hard to build homes with safe water supplies and waste disposal systems. This improves not only the environment, but also the health of people living in these communities.

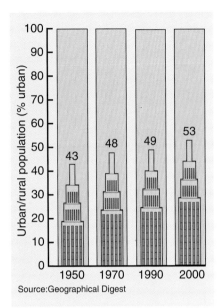

Source:Geographical Digest

▲ *This graph shows how South Africa's urban population has grown since the end of apartheid.*

▼ *These men are working on a project to improve the sewage system in Hankey, Eastern Cape.*

Garbage is also a major environmental problem in urban areas. In many of the poorest settlements, such as shanty towns and some former townships, household waste is not collected. It can build up into hazardous dumps that attract rats and can encourage the spread of disease. Many communities burn garbage, but this creates large amounts of smoke, which can be poisonous if the garbage contains plastics or chemicals. The government has increased garbage collection in recent years, and many urban areas now have recycling centers or collection plans.

► *Emissions from a chemical factory near Port Elizabeth. Air pollution from South Africa's expanding industries is a growing problem.*

IN THEIR OWN WORDS

"I'm Grace (in the purple hat) and I live in a township called Rini, just outside Grahamstown. Around here, plastic bags are a big waste problem. Garbage collection is not good. The bags are light and the wind blows them all over the town. You can see them stuck against fences and bushes; during the rains they can block the drains and cause flooding. My friends and I decided to do something about this problem. We cut the bags into strips and use them for weaving. We make many beautiful things to sell—like this hat I'm holding. It provides us with a good income and has also reduced the problem of garbage in our neighborhood."

6

The Changing Population

A Mixed Population

South Africa's population is made up of black, white, Coloreds, and Asian people. Blacks are by far the biggest group—76 percent of the total. The black population is also increasing the fastest. Although white people controlled South Africa until 1994, they make up just 11 percent of the population, and their population is growing the slowest. In the future, Coloreds will probably overtake them to become the second-biggest racial group. "Colored" is a term that was used by the apartheid government to describe people of mixed ancestry, most often white and East Indian. Coloreds currently make up approximately 9 percent of the population. The term "Asian" refers to people of Indian ancestry. Asians are about 3 percent of the population.

Almost 60 percent of the white population lives in Gauteng or Western Cape—the main economic centers. Almost 40 percent of the black population lives in the former homeland provinces of Kwazulu Natal and Eastern Cape.

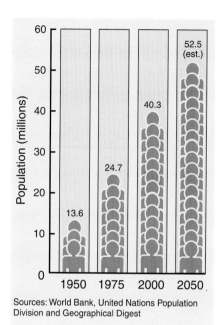

Sources: World Bank, United Nations Population Division and Geographical Digest

▲ *South Africa's population has tripled since 1950.*

IN THEIR OWN WORDS

"My name is Joshua and I live with my wife in Eastern Cape. We have lived here all our lives. We have a small garden and keep chickens and goats. We used to live very well, but now we are too old. We cannot work as well and life is much harder. Our children have all moved to Cape Town, which is nearly 621 miles (1,000 km) away. We get some money from the government and our children send us some when they can. I miss their help though—like today, when I am trying to mend this shed for my goats. We used to have a cow too, but we are no longer strong enough to look after it so we had to sell it."

A Healthier Population

In the year 2000, South Africa's population was over 40 million, compared to just under 25 million in 1975. Today it is still growing, but the speed of growth is much slower. The population is only expected to increase to 52.5 million by 2050. This sudden slowdown is mainly due to the impact of HIV/AIDS (see pages 28–29), but it is also the result of women having fewer children than before. In 1975 women had an average of five children each, but today they have just three.

In 1970, 108 of every 1,000 children died before their fifth birthday, but improved healthcare has reduced this to 65 per 1,000 today. For black children, however, it is still as high as 200 per 1,000, showing that there is yet much to do. Since 1994 the government has made healthcare one of its priorities. It spends 20 percent of its health budget on basic healthcare projects such as opening clinics in rural areas. Special efforts are being made to reduce the number of babies and young children who die. Free healthcare is now available for all pregnant women and for children under six years of age.

▼ *Children in a slum area of Soweto. Poverty and lack of job opportunities make it difficult for black families to leave the townships.*

◄ *This rural family is preparing a healthy meal, but many families have very poor diets. Malnutrition is a major problem, especially for young children.*

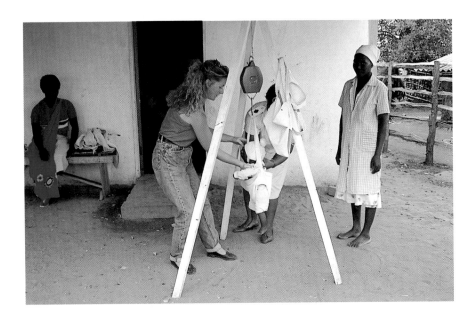

◀ *Health clinics monitor the growth and health of young children. Foreign aid agencies help the government run many of these centers.*

Improving Education

During the apartheid years, most schools and universities were strictly segregated. White people received a much higher standard of education than black people. In 1996 almost 25 percent of blacks over the age of twenty had

▼ *Education is important for adults as well as children. Many did not have the opportunity to study when they were growing up during apartheid.*

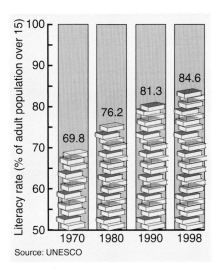

no school education, compared to just 1 percent of whites. Today most schools are open to children of any race. Education is seen as a way of providing people with the knowledge and skills they need to escape poverty and build a more equal society. However, there are still variations in the quality of schools and resources. Rural schools in areas where blacks live are the worst equipped.

A Youthful Population

Like many African countries, South Africa is very youthful. About 42 percent of its population are under 18 years of age, and only 7 percent are over 60. As these young people marry and have families of their own, the total population will continue to grow. The large number of young people also puts more pressure on schools, which are often overcrowded and short of materials, especially in rural areas.

Source: UNESCO

▲ *The proportion of adults who can read and write is increasing slowly but steadily.*

IN THEIR OWN WORDS

"My name is Agnes and I am in charge of this daycare center near Giyani, close to Kruger National Park. We look after young preschool children while their parents work on their farms or in nearby towns. We have many children, but this is only a small number of the children who would like to come here. The problem is that we do not have space for them all; we cannot keep up with the demand. Some parents are too poor to pay the small fees we charge for looking after the nursery and giving the children lunch. Many of the poorest arrived here as refugees from nearby Mozambique during the war there. They came through Kruger and some even tell stories about people being eaten by lions on the way!"

The Threat of HIV/AIDS

HIV/AIDS is a very serious problem in several African countries and it affects about 20 percent of people in South Africa. Lack of education about how the disease is passed on, poor hygiene, and limited healthcare facilities have all helped HIV/AIDS to spread through the population.

This disease is a major threat to South Africa's population and the biggest cause of change. Without HIV/AIDS, the population would probably reach 52 million by 2015, but instead it is expected to remain similar to the current level. This means that 8.5 million people will have been lost due to HIV/AIDS. Many of those dying are young adults or children and, because of this, the average life expectancy is falling. A child born in 1999, for example, could expect to live for 56 years, but a child born in 2015 is likely to live only until the age of 47—nearly 10 years less!

▲ *South Africa's graveyards are filling up fast; many victims of HIV/AIDS are young people.*

HIV is changing family life, too. Many children are becoming orphans following their parents' death and are being sent to live with grandparents or other relatives who can care for them. Some families are now made up of grandparents and grandchildren, with no adults old enough and fit enough to earn money. Poor elderly people are given a pension by the government, but this is not enough to support a whole family, and if they were to die, the children would be left with nothing. Orphanages and care centers are also being built, but the most important task is to reduce the number of people being infected with HIV/AIDS.

▲ *This nurse works at a center for children with HIV/AIDS.*

IN THEIR OWN WORDS

"I am Lukhona and I am 15 years old. I go to school and would like to be a teacher. The schools here are very crowded and we need more teachers. The biggest problem, though, is AIDS. They call it 'slim' here because you lose weight when you are ill with AIDS. Many of my friends have lost their parents because of slim, but I have been lucky. I am frightened about the future though. We do not have good healthcare and many people do not know they are infected. In school we learn all about AIDS and how to protect ourselves. I want to teach people about this horrible disease so we will be able to stop it in the future."

7

Changes at Home

During the apartheid years, there were great differences between the home lives of white people and the home lives of people of other races, especially black people. White people had the best land and the best homes. They had better access to services such as health and education, too. Black people were crowded into special areas known as "homelands" in rural areas or "townships" in urban areas. Houses in these areas were of poor quality and often lacked basic services such as water and electricity supplies. The service provided by local schools and hospitals was not as good as in the white areas and there were not enough schools and hospitals for all the people who needed to use them.

Many black people left the homelands to look for work but most were not allowed to buy or rent homes in the towns and cities. They were forced to build temporary homes on land that did not belong to them. These illegal settlements were known as "shanty towns" or "squatter settlements." They were made up of hundreds of "shacks" barely bigger than a garden shed and had very few services.

IN THEIR OWN WORDS

"My name is Monde and I have just finished a degree in geography at Fort Hare University. My family is not well off and my parents are farm workers in a poor rural area. I am the first from my family to go to college—before the end of apartheid it was difficult for black people like me to get a university education. Poverty is still a big problem, however, and many parents cannot afford to send their children to college. I was lucky because I got a grant from the government. I am now working as a researcher at Rhodes University in Grahamstown, looking at environmental problems affecting soil and water quality."

▶ *An aerial view of a Johannesburg suburb. The people who live here are mainly middle class and white.*

◀ *An aerial view of Soweto near Johannesburg. This was one of the townships where black people were forced to live during apartheid. Today it is still home to thousands of black families.*

Local councils frequently bulldozed shanty towns, claiming they were a health hazard because of the lack of toilets and clean water.

New Beginnings?

People now have the legal right to live where they wish, but the enormous gap in wealth between whites and blacks means that in practice little has changed. Most black people cannot afford to live like an average white person. If anything, the inequality between black and white people is increasing. Some of the more educated black people have been able to take advantage of new opportunities and improve their home lives, but the majority are still living in poverty, with few opportunities available for their families. The scale of the inequality is easiest to understand if we look at the difference between a typical white home and a typical black home.

Different Homes, Different Lives

Most white people live in cities and enjoy a lifestyle similar to that of North Americans or Europeans. They have large, well-built houses with services such as electricity, piped water, and flushing toilets. Most have gardens; some may even have swimming pools. White children are generally healthy and receive a good education. Most can go on to higher education if they wish. Their parents have well-paying jobs and each family has at least one car, as well as modern consumer goods such as computers, mobile phones, and satellite television. They might enjoy going out to the movies or for a meal and they shop in the city-center shopping malls, which are among the best in the world.

For most blacks, home life is very different. While some townships now have services, over half of all black people's homes have no electricity or flushing toilets and nearly three-quarters have no piped water. Most of these homes with poor facilities are in the former homelands. Over a third of black adults are unemployed. Many children receive a poor standard of education, with relatively few continuing into higher education. Most families have only basic possessions; some may even struggle to provide enough food for everyone.

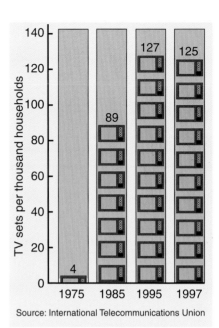

Source: International Telecommunications Union

▲ *TV ownership has increased rapidly, but many of the poorest households still do not have television sets.*

◀ *A modern shopping mall in Johannesburg. Relatively few black people could afford a spending spree here.*

◄ *A home in a shanty town near Grahamstown. The family used any building materials they could find.*

The Colored and Asian populations were also treated differently from whites under apartheid. Today their living standards are generally higher than those of the black population, but lower than those of the white population.

IN THEIR OWN WORDS

"My name is Nelson and today is a public holiday for the local elections. Because we are not working, my sisters and I have decided to repair our home. We use local earth and mix it with water to make a thick mud paste. Then we smear it on to the outside walls of the house and it bakes hard in the sun. It forms a strong wall and protects us from the wind, sun, and rain, but we have to repair it every few years. One day I would like to live in a brick or concrete home like the 'Mandela homes' the government is building in the towns, but there is a long waiting list."

Improving Home Lives

In 1994 the new government promised to reduce the inequalities between black and white people. They planned to improve services such as water and electricity supplies to poor homes and build millions of new houses for people without proper homes. People who had been forced by the apartheid government to leave their own land and move to the homelands were supposed to get their land back. The government also planned improvements in health and education.

However, improving millions of lives is hard, slow work; and progress has been mixed. Between 1994 and 1999, the government managed to build 491,000 homes and helped to pay for a further 630,000. But the need for homes increased to over 2.5 million. In schools some 10,000 classrooms have been built or repaired and 5 million children receive school meals under the successful Primary School Nutrition Program. Yet classrooms are still too crowded (especially in the townships) and students lack books and other resources.

▼ *These are "Mandela homes," which are being built in the Western Cape as part of a government plan to provide better housing. There is a long waiting list for houses like this.*

Rising Crime

Inequality remains a major problem. The rich (mainly white people) are becoming richer while the poor (mainly black people) continue to become poorer. In fact, South Africa is the second most unequal society in the world, after Brazil. One result of this inequality has been an increase in crime, as those who are desperately poor struggle to survive. Some reports even suggest that South Africa is the most dangerous country in the world, with a murder every 29 minutes! The government and tourist authorities are concerned that fear of crime will scare away foreign tourists.

▲ *Fear of violent crime has led many wealthy people to protect themselves behind high walls with dogs and security patrols to keep them safe.*

IN THEIR OWN WORDS

"My name is Catherine (*left*). I'm 12 and I live in Grahamstown. The school that I go to is for girls only and during apartheid it was only open to white children. Today, however, my school is a mixed-race school and I have friends from all different backgrounds. I don't understand why people are treated differently because of their color—I think it's wrong. Many adults still talk about racial problems, but my friends and I don't really think about such things. I hope that when my children grow up everyone will have the same opportunities in life, whatever their background."

◀ *A Ndebele woman displays some of the pots that she has made. With the increase in tourism, women now sell some of their pots as souvenirs.*

Traditions

South Africa's population is made up of a variety of ethnic groups and this variety is reflected in South African culture. European and North American influences are increasing, but local cultures and traditions still survive. The Ndebele people, for example, live in brightly colored huts that are repainted each year by the women.

IN THEIR OWN WORDS

"I am a *Sangoma* and I live in Northern province. A Sangoma is a traditional healer and fortune teller and we help cure local people of their illnesses and advise them in planning their futures. I use natural materials such as shells, bones, and herbs to help me in my work. For example, to tell a fortune I shake the shells in my hand and then look at the way they land. The pattern tells me what the person's future will be. Today many people use doctors and lawyers but in poor and rural communities Sangomas like myself are still important and well respected. My people have followed beliefs like this for hundreds of years and it is important that such traditions continue."

One of the most famous cultures is that of the Zulu people, who have a reputation as fierce warriors. Today they perform dances and tell stories to keep their culture alive, both for their own people and also as a popular tourist attraction.

Religion

Religion plays an important part in the life of local communities. Christianity is the main religion, with Protestant and black independent churches being the biggest groups. However, traditional African beliefs are still followed by almost 30 percent of people. Most of the Asians living in South Africa are Hindus but there is a smaller group of Muslims. Some of the Colored community living around Cape Town are also Muslims.

Sports

Sports are very popular, with rugby and cricket being two sports that South Africa is particularly good at. During apartheid South Africa was banned from international competition, but in 1995 it marked its return to world sports by hosting and winning the Rugby World Cup.

Since 1994 there have been greater opportunities for all races to enjoy both watching and taking part in sports. Soccer is particularly popular among the black population, with most communities having some kind of soccer program. But rugby and cricket, which were traditionally supported only by white people, are beginning to attract more black and Colored fans. The national sides now have some very talented black and Colored players on their teams.

▼ *A game of street hockey in Cape Town. Black children had few opportunities to play organized sports under apartheid. Now the situation is slowly improving.*

8

Changes at Work

An African Giant

Many African countries rely heavily on cash crops such as coffee, or minerals such as diamonds, for their income. South Africa, however, produces many different goods and services. This is partly because many countries refused to trade with South Africa during apartheid. South Africa was forced to develop its economy in order to be self sufficient. It has rich natural resources and a skilled workforce, and today it has the strongest economy in Africa.

Changing Opportunities

The end of apartheid brought new opportunities for South African companies, which were now able to trade with other countries. More people were able to find jobs in the tourist industry, as large numbers of foreign tourists began to visit. The food and drink industry also expanded. South African wine exports, for example, nearly tripled between 1993 and 1995, to 18,760,000 gallons (71 million liters) per year.

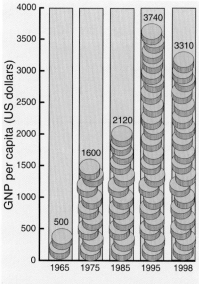

Source: World Bank

▲ *The amount of money South Africa earns from the goods it produces has more than doubled since 1975.*

IN THEIR OWN WORDS

"I'm Andrew (*right*) and I own an ostrich farm at Oudtshoorn, in Western Cape. The land is very dry around here and not much good for growing crops but in the late 18th and early 19th centuries a number of ostrich farms were set up. They provided feathers for the fashion industry in Europe. Today we farm ostriches for their meat—it's a healthy alternative to beef and very tasty! Around ten years ago I opened my farm for tourists. They can feed the birds and if they are feeling very brave they can even try riding an ostrich!"

However, South African companies also faced greater competition from abroad and about half a million people have lost their jobs as a result. The mining industry has suffered more than most, with an estimated 250,000 miners losing their jobs between 1987 and 1997. In 1999 about 36 percent of people were unemployed, although the levels varied greatly from place to place. In some former homelands, up to 80 percent of people may be unemployed, particularly in areas that used to supply workers to the mines. There are also variations linked to race and gender. In 1999 black women had the highest unemployment rate, while white men were the most likely to find work.

▲ *A research scientist at work in a chemistry lab in Johannesburg. The end of apartheid has brought new opportunities for educated black people.*

▼ *A machinist in a textile factory in Johannesburg. Unemployment is high among black women, and many have moved to the cities to find work.*

◄ *These unemployed men and women are taking part in a government plan to help them get back to work. Here they are learning how to make cinder blocks.*

Government Support

Since the end of apartheid the government has been trying to encourage foreign businesses and industries to invest in South Africa. It has been trying to encourage local people to start their own businesses, too. In 1996 it introduced a new policy—the Growth, Employment and Redistribution (GEAR) strategy—which it hoped would help. The idea was to keep wages low and remove taxes and other regulations from businesses.

IN THEIR OWN WORDS

"My name is Hazel, I'm 32 and I live in Virginia in Free State province, though I'm originally from North-West province. I didn't complete my schooling and had very few skills when I started work. I could only get poorly paying jobs and it was very difficult to support my two children. In 1994 a training center was set up to train unemployed women in spinning and weaving to make rugs and blankets. I was lucky to get a place and learned how to use the looms, as I'm doing here. I now have a regular wage and have just started training school dropouts who have joined the center."

IN THEIR OWN WORDS

"My name is Cornwell (I'm the one sitting down, in the white shirt) and I am 17 years old. I have recently started learning metalwork at a center in Mossel Bay. Unemployment is very bad at the moment and if you don't have skills, it's even harder to find work. One day I hope that the skills I'm learning here will allow me to start my own business and provide other people with jobs. The government gives small grants to people with ideas for businesses and I'm hoping to get a grant in the future."

GEAR was expected to boost the economy and create up to 400,000 jobs per year, but unfortunately it has not been as successful as was hoped. Very few new jobs have been created and workers have been protesting against poor pay. In 1998 an estimated three million working days were lost due to strikes. Successes such as a new aluminum plant at Richards Bay have helped the economy but provided few jobs, because machinery is now used to do a lot of the work, instead of people.

Training and Work Programs

New ideas have been introduced to try to help those who have the most difficulty finding work. Government programs provide unemployed people with jobs building roads or digging drainage ditches. One such plan is the "Working for Water" project. People are given work clearing vegetation from streams and rivers so that more water can reach storage reservoirs. By the end of 1998, this plan had improved water supplies and provided work for 42,000 people.

Plans were announced to provide more strategies like the Working for Water project, but the plans were criticized for teaching few skills and providing only temporary employment. In 1998 the Skills Development Act was passed. This puts greater emphasis on developing people's skills through long-term training. The government hopes that this will improve people's chances of finding permanent jobs in the future, or even help them to create their own jobs by setting up new businesses.

Many of the new job opportunities depend on investments from private companies, but in the very poorest parts of the country, the government is also playing its part. In the St. Lucia area of Kwazulu Natal, for example, the government is working with private companies to encourage tourism development around the state-owned wetlands. Guest houses are being built to provide accommodations for 5,500 tourists and other facilities are being improved. The project will create at least 2,000 new jobs.

▼ *This man has recently opened his own shoe making and repair business. His shop is in a unit that was built by the government to provide premises for new businesses.*

Subsistence Workers

The poorest people, living in former homelands, work as subsistence farmers, trying to grow enough food for their families. In recent years, though, many farmers have started growing more valuable crops, such as sunflowers or sugar cane. These are called "cash crops" because they are sold for money to buy food and other supplies.

Government experts help train farmers to grow these new crops. Some farmers are also given help by companies that agree to buy their crop when it is harvested. Subsistence and cash-crop farmers face great risks every year because of the unpredictable weather. In 1998 and 1999, the weather was unusually dry and harvests were smaller than normal. In 2000 unusually wet weather caused flood damage to crops in some areas.

◀ *After a good harvest, subsistence farmers may have a few surplus crops. Women often sell the produce from road stands, like these in Fort Beaufort, Eastern Cape.*

IN THEIR OWN WORDS

"My name is Patience and I live in Mpumalanga province on a large commercial farm close to Swaziland. The company has given me a house and my children can go to the local school for free. The farm grows tropical fruit such as mangoes and papayas for export to European supermarkets. Today we are preparing papayas for shipping. First they are cleaned and then they are waxed and packed into plastic crates with leaves to help protect them on their journey. We work long days during the harvest season and it can be very tiring, but I am lucky to have regular work and I feel the company looks after me and my family."

9

The Way Ahead

The Speed of Change

South Africa's government and people still have much to do if they are to turn the hopes and dreams of the "Rainbow Nation" into reality. Everyone, especially the black community, had very high expectations after Nelson Mandela's election in 1994. Some people now complain that they are no better off, and in fact may even be worse off than before. Unemployment is high, and poverty and inequality are still major problems.

There is no doubt that some have benefited. A small group of well-educated blacks, Coloreds, and Asians have been able to take advantage of new opportunities, and their quality of life has improved dramatically. But millions of others still suffer from poverty and a lack of opportunities. For these people there has been little change.

IN THEIR OWN WORDS

"My name is Otto (*right*) and I am the mayor of Hankey. I am proud to represent my people and to be involved in building a new future for South Africa, in which every person has the same opportunities. In my community we are investing in training young people to set up their own businesses. We are also improving local housing, health, and education. I hope to be elected again so that I can bring further benefits to my community. Some people believe the benefits of majority rule are not yet visible, but we must work for them ourselves. The government cannot undo fifty years of apartheid overnight!"

Hope for the Future

Yet there is hope. South Africans are optimistic about their future, and the new freedom that is shared by all is leading to success stories across the country.

◄ *Building a community center in Fairbairn. Projects like these are helping to improve the lives of poor people all over South Africa.*

South Africa is becoming a major world trader, too. It has a growing role in leading all of southern Africa in the global economy.

Most important of all, however, is that South Africa's children are learning to live, play, study, and work side by side. A South Africa free of racial conflict is the most important change for both the present day and the future —and it is a change being led by today's children.

IN THEIR OWN WORDS

"We are the children of the new South Africa and together we are working for a more equal and fair society. Today we play sports together, we visit each other's homes and we learn about our country and history together. We know there is still much work to be done, but we are making a start, and we think that working together is the most important thing to do. South Africa is a beautiful country with lots of opportunities. We hope that when our children reach our age our goals will have been met and all South Africans will be able to look ahead to a bright future."

Glossary

Acid rain Rain produced when sulphur dioxide and nitrogen oxides (gases released when fuels are burned) dissolve in rainwater to fall as sulphuric or nitric acid.

Agriculture The use of land to produce crops for food or other uses (e.g. cotton for use in the textile industry).

Apartheid A word meaning "to keep apart." It is used to describe the separation of white and black people in South Africa between 1948 and 1994.

Cash crops Crops that are grown to be sold, rather than to provide food for the farmer. They include crops such as coffee, sugarcane, and oranges.

Charcoal Wood that has been partially burned, but without air, so that it does not catch fire and burn up. It can then be used as a cleaner and more efficient fuel than wood for cooking or heating.

Coloreds A term used in South Africa to describe people of mixed ancestry (usually East Indian and white).

Culture The beliefs, customs, language, and behavior shared by a group of people. It can include certain foods, music, art, clothes, and stories, for example.

Cyclone A tropical storm with very strong winds and heavy rains. Cyclones are known as hurricanes and typhoons in some parts of the world.

Drought A long period of below-average rainfall that can lead to crop failures and water shortages.

Economy The total amount of goods and services provided or used by a particular area (e.g. a town or a country). Its size is normally measured in terms of money.

Emissions Waste material released into the natural environment (e.g. waste gases from factory chimneys).

Eroded Erosion is a process in which something becomes worn (eroded). It is normally caused by the action of wind or water.

Exports Products and services sold to foreign countries (e.g., fruit and wine sold by South Africa to European countries).

Fertile Full of nutrients and good for growing crops.

Fossil fuels Fuels formed over millions of years from the fossilized remains of plants and animals. They include coal, oil, and natural gas.

GNP per capita GNP is Gross National Product, the amount of money South Africa makes from all the goods and services it produces. Per capita means "per person." GNP per capita is the total amount of money earned, divided by the total population.

Government pass A booklet giving personal details such as your name and address and information about your employer.

Gullying Cracks in the ground that become enlarged over time (by erosion) and form gullies.

HIV/AIDS Human Immunodeficiency Virus (HIV) is a virus spread by unprotected sex, or by infected needles or blood supplies. It can develop into Acquired Immunodeficiency Syndrome (AIDS), when the immune system is weakened and cannot fight off a number of illnesses that can be fatal.

Homeland A rural area in which black people were forced to live during the apartheid period.

Hydroelectric power Electricity generated by water as it passes through turbines. These are normally built into large dams across river valleys.

Invest Put money into a business.

Irrigation Using sprinklers or water channels to supply water to crops to make up for low or unpredictable rainfall.

Majority rule Rule by the biggest ethnic group in a country.

Population The total number of people living in a particular area such as a town or country.

Segregated Separated according to racial group or some other factor, such as religion.

Shanty towns Makeshift settlements close to urban centers. They normally lack basic services and are often built illegally.

Solar power Electricity generated by converting the energy from the sun using solar panels. It is a clean and renewable form of energy.

Subsistence farming Farming that provides food mainly for the household. Surplus food may be sold.

Townships Urban areas that housed black people during apartheid. They were normally located on the edges of major cities, such as Soweto outside Johannesburg.

Tropical Very hot, with high rainfall.

Further Information

Books

Flint, David. *Modern Industrial World: South Africa*. London: Hodder Wayland, 1996.

Middleton, Nick. *Country Fact Files: Southern Africa*. London: Hodder Wayland, 1995.

Nagle, Garret. *Country Studies: South Africa*. Westport, CT: Heinemann, 1998.

Sparks, Allister. *Tomorrow Is Another Country: The Inside Story of South Africa's Road to Change*. Chicago: University of Chicago Press, 1996.

Thompson, Leonard. *A History of South Africa*. New Haven, CT: Yale University Press, 1996.

Fodor's Exploring South Africa. New York: Fodor's, 2001.

Eyewitness Travel Guides: South Africa. New York: DK Publishing, 1999.

Video

Explore the music of South Africa, tour famous sites and be guided through a game parks in these suggested videos:

South Africa 2000

Going Places—South Africa;

South Africa: Diary;

South African Safari.

Useful Addresses

South African Embassy
3051 Massachusetts Avenue NW
Washington, D.C. 20008

South African Tourism
500 Fifth Avenue, Suite 2040
New York, NY 10110
(800) 822-5368
(202) 232-4400

Websites

http://www.gov.za
The South African government website contains a great deal of information about the country and government policies and links to many related websites.

http://www.sas.upenn.edu/African_Studies/ Country_Specific/S-Africa.html
South Africa Page
Collection of resources from the University of Pennsylvania's African Studies Center including a map, travel advisories, and reviewed links.

http://www.southafrica.net
Official Tourism site

http://www.statssa.gov.za
Statistics South Africa
This government agency publishes the country's official statistics.

http://www-sul.stanford.edu
(search: South Africa)
Africa South of the Sahara
General and regional indexes cover a broad range of topics, from art to weather. Maintained by the African Studies Association at Stanford Univ.

Index

Page numbers in **bold** refer to photographs, maps or statistics panels.